ROTTWEILER:
THE ROTTWEILER
BIBLE

Rottweiler Complete Guide

INCLUDES: ROTTWEILER PUPPIES, ROTTWEILER ADULTS,
ROTTWEILER CARE, ROTTWEILER BREEDERS,
ROTTWEILER HEALTH, TRAINING & MORE!

By Mark Manfield

DYM Worldwide Publishers

ISBN: 978-1-911355-32-8

Copyright © **DYM Worldwide Publishers, 2017.** 2 Lansdowne Row, Number 240, London. W1J 6HL.

Table of Contents

CHAPTER 1

Introducing the Rottweiler!

Just because the Rottweiler is a big, muscular breed doesn't mean that these dogs don't have a heart of gold. I can personally attest to the fact that the Rottweiler breed is as friendly, loving, and goofy as they come! Although these dogs have a reputation for being guard dogs and watchdogs, they also make great family pets. If this is new information to you, then you have a lot to learn about Rottweiler dogs!

I am the adoring owner of a Rottweiler myself, and Rusty has been my loyal friend and companion for five years now. I adopted him as a puppy and we have grown together over the years, and our friendship has grown stronger with each passing day. I can confidently say that I don't know where my life would be without Rusty in it, and I am certain that I don't want to find out!

You may be thinking of getting a Rottweiler, or already have one, but aren't sure how to ensure it has the best behavior, is well behaved, obedient, or how you can keep it healthy and make sure it lives the longest and healthiest life possible. Rottweilers are an amazing breed, but I must admit that they aren't the right choice for everyone. These dogs grow large and they can sometimes be a handful when it comes to training and socialization. If you are willing to put in the time and effort, however, it is worth it. In this book I'm going to teach you techniques which make sure your Rottweiler's behavior is under control, and a pleasure to deal with. You will then be equipped with all you need to have a Rottweiler, and maximize your experience and your Rottweiler's experience throughout the journey. Once you form a bond with your Rottweiler dog, you will have his love and loyalty for life. With the knowledge in this book, you can be sure you'll be completely prepared and equipped for the responsibility and rewards of this magnificent breed. Not only will he be your friend, but he will be your protector as well. There is nothing he won't do for you! In this book you will even learn how to ensure your Rottweiler is with you as long as possible, and what you can do to improve his chances at living the longest lifespan possible. I'm about to empower you fully to have a well behaved, well-trained, healthy, and happy Rottweiler.

If you are reading this book, I think it is safe to assume that you are interested in the Rottweiler breed, or want to further enhance your knowledge. Perhaps you have already had some experience with these dogs, or maybe you are completely new. Whatever the case, this book is the perfect place for you to start your search for Rottweiler info, or to develop a deeper understanding of how to care for your dog and optimize the experience throughout his life. I couldn't be happier with my Rottweiler, and it is my goal to help you determine whether this breed could be the perfect match for you as well! If you are an experienced Rottweiler owner, this guide will give you the secrets that long time breeders and owners have come to recognize are most important for the breed. My name is Mark Manfield, and over the years I've owned and trained many dogs, and spent many months specifically with Rottweiler owners and breeders, ensuring the best of their valuable wisdom is available here to you in a convenient and easy to use format.

The big, bold, and beautiful Rottweiler is unmistakable!

There is a lot of Rottweiler info you need to know before you decide whether this is the right breed for you and your family. For one thing, you need to know about the background of the breed, to understand the Rottweiler's temperament. You will learn how to prevent disobedience, greatly reduce the likelihood of any aggression, excessive barking, potty accidents, and many other issues that really are preventable if you know how. You should also learn the basics about how much exercise and space these dogs require, and what kind of food is best for them. How to ensure you give them the healthy lifestyle which will allow them to live the longest possible life. You will find all this information and more within the pages of this comprehensive Rottweiler guide.

People thank me for how my tips have helped them build a stronger and more rewarding life with their dog. These are the exact principles I will be unveiling to you in this guide. I will cover topics ranging from general Rottweiler info to detailed tips for raising and training your Rottweiler puppy or dog. The result of this will be an obedient Rottweiler who feels happy and secure with you, and has friendly and dependable good behavior. I will tell you everything you need to know to choose a responsible Rottweiler breeder, and how to prepare your home and family for a new addition. I'll also cover practical topics like nutrition, training, breeding, grooming, and more – what more could you possibly ask for?

On the run! Rottweiler puppies are an absolute pleasure –
they are full of boundless energy and have endless love to give!

The Rottweiler is a beautiful and wonderful breed, but owning this kind of dog comes with a unique set of challenges. Not only do you have to deal with the training and socialization of your Rottweiler puppy, but you may also have to deal with the stigma against the Rottweiler breed that many people harbor. Treat this book as your ultimate Rottweiler owners guide and you will know by the time you finish reading it whether a Rottweiler is the right dog for you and whether you can handle the challenges of being a Rottweiler owner. With the wisdom of Rottweiler owners and breeders used to create this guide, you will be well-equipped to succeed with your Rottweiler too. It's very important you read and understand what's within this book right now - so you don't miss out on your window of opportunity, when your Rottweiler's personality and health profile is developing. Your Rottweiler's brain, body, and temperament develop quickly, so the faster you can apply what's in this book, the better your Rottweiler will turn out.

The Rottweiler guidance and insider tips you are about to read in this book are proven to produce incredible results for Rottweiler owners. Every chapter in this book will provide you with actionable steps that will help you instill good behaviors in your Rottweiler, make sure he is healthy and happy, prevent aggression, and take your dog anywhere and show him off to everyone you meet with confidence. It was my goal to create the complete Rottweiler guide book for prospective Rottweiler owners, and also those experienced with the breed. If you are ready to learn more about the Rottweiler breed, or to maximize what you already know and build on that, turn the page and keep reading!

CHAPTER 2

Rottweiler Dogs: The German Rottweiler in History

You probably already know that domestic dogs are descended from wild wolves, but if that is the case why do modern dogs look so different from wolves? The answer to this question comes from the fact that wild wolves were domesticated somewhere between 8,000 and 12,000 years ago. That is a long time! Between then and now, domesticated dogs have spread throughout the world, originally by nomadic human populations, and selectively bred for various characteristics by individual populations.

The Development of the German Rottweiler

Compared to early domesticated dogs, the Rottweiler dog is a fairly new breed but its origins still go all the way back to the Roman Empire. Though you may be more familiar with the Rottweiler as a guard dog, it is actually one of the oldest herding breeds in the world. There is evidence to suggest that the ancestors of the Rottweiler were ancient Roman drover dogs – dogs of the mastiff-type that were tough and dependable with solid intelligence and strong guarding instincts. As the ancient Romans traveled across the continent, they brought their herds of cattle with them along with the dogs they used to herd the animals and to keep watch over them at night.

The town of Rottweil, Germany is located in Southwest Germany in the state of Baden-Württemberg.

Sometime around 74 A.D., the Roman army traversed across the Alps into what is now known as southern Germany. There, the Roman drover dogs were used for the next two centuries for herding and guarding cattle. At some point, a town in that region was named Rottweil and it became significant as a trade center. Around that same time, Roman drover dogs came to be adopted by traveling butchers to carry and guard pouches of money. These dogs were eventually named butcher dogs or, in German, Rottweiler Metzgerhunds.

During the 1800s, railroads were developed as the primary method of transporting livestock so the need for livestock guarding breeds like the Rottweiler declined. In fact, the German Rottweiler declined in numbers so severely that there was just one specimen of the breed available for a dog show held in Heilbronn. It wasn't until World War I that the Rottweiler dog breed experienced a revival as the need for police dogs increased. Rottweilers were given jobs as messenger dogs, ambulance dogs, draught dogs, and guard dogs in both the first and second World Wars.

With his strength and intelligence, the Rottweiler is a very versatile breed. He has been used for everything from herding and livestock guarding to police work and more!

In 1914, the Deutscher Rottweiler Klub (DRK), or the German Rottweiler Club, was formed in Germany. The following year, the Süddeutscher Rottweiler Klub (SDRK), the South German Rottweiler Club), was formed. Together, these two clubs helped to revive the Rottweiler breed, though they had very different goals. For example, the DRK set out to develop the Rottweiler as a working breed. The Allgemeiner Deutscher Rottweiler Klub (ADRK) was formed from an amalgamation of various breed clubs in 1924, and it is currently recognized worldwide as the home club of the Rottweiler breed.

The Rottweiler is a strong and proud breed known for its natural guarding instincts. It is also a talented herding breed!

The Modern Rottweiler Breed

In 1931, the American Kennel Club officially recognized the Rottweiler and accepted it for show. The breed was first exhibited at the Crufts dog show in Britain in 1936, though the breed's popularity didn't really take off until the mid-1990s. In fact, the Rottweiler even ranked as the most registered dog by the AKC. In recent years, however, the Rottweiler breed has fallen in the ranks, taking the 9th slot in the year 2013. In 2015, the Rottweiler was ranked as the 9th most popular dog breed according to AKC registration.

Although there is no mistaking a Rottweiler dog when you see one, various dog breed organizations breed the Rottweiler to slightly different standards. For the most part, however, these clubs agree on certain characteristics such as the breed's size, strength, and body composition. To give you an idea of what the perfect Rottweiler dog would look like, consider the following excerpt from the AKC Rottweiler Breed Standard:

"The Rottweiler is a medium large, robust and powerful dog, black with clearly defined rust markings. His compact and substantial build denotes great strength, agility and endurance. Dogs are characteristically more massive throughout with larger frame and heavier bone than bitches. Bitches are distinctly feminine, but without weakness of substance or structure."

This excerpt gives you a general idea of what the Rottweiler breed should look like overall, but the breed standard goes into much greater detail if you keep reading. The American Kennel Club standard states that an adult Rottweiler dog should stand 24 to 27 inches (62 to 68 cm) tall and a female Rottweiler should stand 22 to 25 inches (56 to 63.5 cm) tall. The average weight for the breed is anywhere from 75 pounds to 110 pounds (34 to 50 kg), though a big Rottweiler could weigh even more.

Pictures of Rottweilers

The Rottweiler is a unique and beautiful breed that any dog owner would be lucky to have. With their muscular bodies and dark coats, they can look a bit formidable but these dogs are all heart – they even make great family pets!

Here are some pictures of the Rottweiler breed to show you what I mean when I say that these dogs are gorgeous!

The Rottweiler is easy to identify with his muscular body and characteristic black coat with rust-colored markings.

Rottweilers are known as much for their muscular build as for their natural protective instincts – they make great guard dogs.

Rottweiler puppies are little bundles of energy and love – be careful because they can sometimes be a little too mischievous!

CHAPTER 3

Rottweiler Dog Types and Rottweiler Mixes – How to Tell the Difference

While the Rottweiler is easily one of the most recognizable dog breeds, there are actually a few different types you should be aware of. You may also be interested in various Rottweiler mixed-breeds if you are at all familiar with the recent trend toward "designer dogs". The name "designer dog" is usually given to a mixed breed dog resulting from a cross between two pure breeds like a purebred Rottweiler and a Labrador Retriever.

Before I get into the details about different Rottweiler mix breeds, however, I want to make sure you understand the different types of Rottweilers you may come across as you start looking for a Rottweiler breeder. The first thing you need to know is the difference between a purebred Rottweiler and a non-purebred.

The term "purebred" is defined as, "an animal bred from parents of the same breed or variety". This simply means that a purebred Rottweiler is a dog breed from two Rottweiler parents. It is impossible to have a purebred dog if the parents are two different breeds. When this happens, the resulting litter of puppies are all mixed breed or crossbreed dogs. There is nothing inherently wrong with this, but if you want to show your dog in an AKC or Kennel Club show, he must be a purebred Rottweiler, and you'll have to prove it with pedigree paperwork.

A purebred Rottweiler is a large, impressive dog with a friendly temperament and unwavering loyalty for family.

German Rottweiler vs. American Rottweiler

Another thing you should know about before you start shopping for Rottweiler puppies for sale is the difference between the German Rottweiler and the American Rottweiler. If you think back to the previous chapter about Rottweiler breed history, you will remember that this breed was developed in Germany. Over the past few centuries, however, the breed has spread throughout the world and different breed clubs have popped up in various countries.

Each Rottweiler breed club has its own set of standards for the bred and that's where the real differences lie

To explain things simply, a German Rottweiler is simply a Rottweiler bred in Germany and an American Rottweiler is one bred in the United States. If you dig a little deeper, however, you will come to realize that the Rottweiler breed clubs in each of these countries played a key role in the development of the breed in that area. For example, the Allgemeiner Deutscher Rottweiler Klub in Germany has set standards for the Rottweiler which differ in some ways from the American Kennel Club standards for the Rottweiler in the United States.

Both German and American Rottweilers look very similar in appearance, but there are some differences in breeding. For example, the Allgemeiner Deutscher Rottweiler Klub is more interested in the utility of the breed than in its appearance – this club wants the Rottweiler to have a sharp mind and a mild temperament so that they are well-suited to assisting their human companions. This club puts an emphasis on the Rottweiler as a working breed, fulfilling such roles as companion dogs, guide dogs, and security dogs as well as family pets.

The one major physical trait difference between the German and American Rottweiler is that the German Rottweiler cannot have a docked tail. The AKC standard for the breed requires a docked tail, though there is a movement toward natural tails in Rottweilers kept as pets in the United States. Another physical difference between the two is that the German Rottweiler tends to be a little larger than the American version of the breed.

Although he may be large and muscular, the Rottweiler is not an aggressive breed – he gets along well with other dogs.

What Rottweiler Mix Breeds Are Out There?

The characteristic that makes the Rottweiler dog so recognizable is his black coloration with rust-colored markings. This type of coloration is seen in a number of other breeds like the Doberman Pinscher and the Dachshund. Just because a dog exhibits this coloration doesn't necessarily mean it is related to the Rottweiler breed, but there are some mixed breed dogs that have a distinct Rottweiler-like appearance.

Mixed breed dogs are as diverse as the myriad colors in the rainbow. The size, coloration, and temperament of a mixed breed dog is highly variable depending on the two breeds used in the crossing. Though it is technically possible to create a Rottweiler mix using any other breed, there are a few combinations that are most common. Some examples of common Rottweiler mix breeds include the following:

- Rottweiler Lab Mix
- Rottweiler Mastiff
- Rottweiler Pitbull Mix
- Rottweiler Shepherd Mix

A Labrador Rottweiler crossing could result in a number of different colors since Labs come in chocolate, black, and yellow.

What You Should Know About Rottweiler Mix Puppies

When you cross two purebred dogs, you never know exactly what the results are going to be – this is certainly the case for Rottweiler mix puppies. Many designer dog breeders say that their puppies offer the best of both breeds, but the truth is that you cannot predict which traits the puppy will inherit from both parents. You also cannot predict the adult size of Rottweiler mix puppies, unless they are bred from two similar-sized breeds.

Labrador Rottweiler and Rottweiler Shepherd Mix

The Rottweiler Lab Mix is simply a cross between a male or female Rottweiler and a Labrador Retriever. Because Labs come in three different colors (chocolate, yellow, and black), Labrador Rottweiler mixes come in a wide range of colors. Another popular pairing is the Rottweiler Shepherd mix – a Rottweiler with a German Shepherd. These dogs have similar colorings so that may not change a lot, but the Shepherd has a slightly longer coat and a fluffier tail which may be evident in Rottweiler Shepherd mix puppies.

A Rottweiler Shepherd might have a slightly longer coat with a fluffier tail but it will be similar in size to a traditional Rottweiler.

ROTTWEILER: The Rottweiler Bible

Rottweiler Mastiff and Rottweiler Pitbull Mix

Sometimes when a breeder wants to develop the protective instincts of the Rottweiler breed, he might cross the Rottweiler with another breed known for its protective instincts like a Mastiff or a Pitbull. A Rottweiler Mastiff is a very large dog and, while a Rottweiler Pitbull Mix might be a little smaller, both breeds will exhibit great strength and they will be very protective.

Miniature Rottweiler and Other Variations on the Purebred Rottweiler

In addition to these Rottweiler mix puppies, there are some variations on the Rottweiler breed that you may stumble upon. In very rare cases, you may come across a white Rottweiler – also known as an albino Rottweiler. White is not a color typically seen in the Rottweiler dog breed, but some dogs carry a recessive gene for albinism – this gene stops the melanin (the pigment in your dog's skin) from developing color which results in a dog with no pigment.

White Rottweilers are very rare, and responsible breeders will not breed in favor of this quality because it is frequently paired with serious health problems. It is important to distinguish, however, between an albino Rottweiler and a white Rottweiler mix. If a Rottweiler is bred with a dog that is naturally white in color, it is possible for the Rottweiler mix puppies to be white as well. It all comes down to genetics.

Another type of Rottweiler you may come across in your search is the miniature Rottweiler. I want to caution you heavily against buying a puppy that is labeled a miniature Rottweiler because you really don't know what you are getting. The Rottweiler is a large-breed dog and while a female Rottweiler is smaller than a male, they still weigh 75 pounds or more at maturity. If you come across a dog labeled as a miniature Rottweiler and it weighs less than 50 pounds, the chances are good that it isn't a Rottweiler at all and you may never find out what it actually is.

Be careful about buying a miniature Rottweiler – it may be nothing more than a Rottweiler puppy or another breed entirely!

I want to tell you a story about this. A few years back, before I adopted my Rusty, I came into contact with a friend who had a small Rottweiler of her own. At this point, I was already fairly familiar with the Rottweiler breed, and I knew that they were fairly large dogs. When I met my friend Cindy's dog (his name was Sebastian), I asked her how old he was, thinking that he was still a puppy because he couldn't have weighed more than 40 pounds at the time. Cindy was confused by my question, however, and told me that Sebastian was full-grown. When I asked her how that was possible, she told me he was a miniature Rottweiler. I'll admit that, as skeptical as I was, I thought there was a chance that miniature Rottweilers were a legitimate thing and I just hadn't heard about them. So, I did a little research of my own. Everything I read, however, confirmed what I already knew to be true – that the miniature Rottweiler did not exist. What I did find was an anecdote in an online forum posted by another person who had purchased a so-called miniature Rottweiler. What she found out after pressing the breeder for more details, however, was that her dog wasn't a Rottweiler at all. The dog was a Pug mixed with a Miniature Pinscher, which resulted in a small dog with black and rust-colored markings.

I tell you this story not because I want to make a big deal about my friend's mistake, but to show you how careful you must be when shopping around for a Rottweiler breeder. It is unfortunate but true that there are many hobby breeders out there who take advantage of under-informed dog owners, charging ridiculous prices for what amounts to be a poorly bred puppy. I encourage you to do your research and to only buy from a club-registered breeder if you want a purebred Rottweiler.

CHAPTER 4

Is The Rottweiler the Right Dog For Me?

Rottweiler Temperament, Rottweiler Training, and Rottweiler Space Needs

I have you to be honest with you - the Rottweiler is not the easiest breed to care for. I don't say this to try and scare you away from the breed but I do want you to be completely informed. The last thing I want you to do is to create a false image of the Rottweiler breed in your head only to discover that when you bring your puppy home, he is completely different from what you were expecting. As a dog owner, you need to be practical, and that requires you to do some careful research about the breed before you purchase a puppy – that is the point of this chapter.

In this chapter I am going to tell you everything you need to know about the Rottweiler's temperament as well as his need for space and some training challenges you may encounter. Although I am going to do my best to give you as much detailed and accurate information as I can, I recommend that you read some other Rottweiler training books as well. Training Rottweilers is not the most difficult task in the world, but it certainly isn't the easiest. I just want you to know what you are getting yourself into before you make your final decision.

Rottweiler Temperament – A Good Choice for Families?

The Rottweiler is a big dog – not only can they weigh more than 100 pounds (45 kg) at maturity, but most of that weight is pure muscle. This being the case, the Rottweiler is definitely not a meek and mild breed. Rottweilers are sometimes described as "gentle giants," but you need to be realistic about the temperament of the breed. Not all the same breed have the same temperament – a lot of it has to do with breeding and training. You'll learn more about the challenges of training your Rottweiler later in this chapter.

When properly trained and socialized, the Rottweiler can be very friendly with other dogs as well as other household pets.

For the most part, Rottweilers are affectionate and loving dogs, though many of them become one-person dogs – this simply means that they bond more closely with one member of the family. Rottweiler temperament ranges from quiet and reserved to goofy and fun-loving – it really has to do with how you treat your puppy and how much time you spend developing a bond with him while he is young. When properly trained and socialized, Rottweilers can be fun and friendly dogs.

With their history of livestoc guardianship, you can expect your Rottweiler to have a calm alertness about him. He should not be standoffish, but he will always be aware of his surroundings. These dogs are definitely not nervous or shy, though they may be wary around strangers until they get to know the person. Rottweilers are also known for thinking before they act. These dogs have strong guarding instincts but they are more likely to stand as a physical barrier between you and any threat than they are to rush head-first into a dangerous situation.

In terms of how your Rottweiler is able to get along with other pets and other people, it varies from one case to another. If you raise your Rottweiler from a puppy with consistent training and early socialization, there is no reason why he shouldn't get along with other household pets – he will also get along well with children. But if you fail to exhibit a strong hand in leadership and you don't train your Rottweiler from an early age, you could find yourself dealing with a variety of behavior problems.

Rottweiler Space and Exercise Needs

In addition to considering the Rottweiler's temperament before getting a puppy, you should also think about whether you can provide for this breed's space and exercise needs. According to the AKC, the Rottweiler is a medium-large breed. These dogs can grow to over 100 pounds (45 kg) at maturity so they are definitely not a small dog. For the most part, Rottweilers do not do well in apartments or condos. Not only do they need a lot of indoor space, but they require some outdoor space as well. The Rottweiler is not a high-energy breed, but they are fairly active dogs and they need plenty of daily exercise.

Not only is the Rottweiler a fairly large dog, but they are also a working breed – these dogs do best when they have a job to do. Rottweilers were originally developed as livestock guardians but they performed many other roles as well. The modern Rottweiler can be trained for a variety of dog sports including agility, tracking, carting, flyballfly ball, herding and more. Rottweilers are very smart and they love to learn – just keep in mind that their size and their independent nature comes with some challenges.

The Challenges of Rottweiler Training

Any Rottweiler training book worth its salt will spend some time talking about the temperament of the Rottweiler breed. Though intelligence is certainly an important factor in determining how easy or difficult it is to train a dog, you shouldn't underestimate the importance of temperament. The Rottweiler breed is very smart – he thinks before he reacts and he will take his cues from his owner. This means that the training method you choose, and the way you treat your dog, will have a significant impact on his temperament as well as his training.

Now I want you to take a few minutes to think about what you knew about the Rottweiler breed before you started reading this book. When you pictured a Rottweiler dog, what did you see? Many people, when asked what they know about the Rottweiler, talk about the breed's use as a guard dog. They think of the Rottweiler as a naturally aggressive and protective breed – a dog used to guard property and to deter burglars.

The Rottweiler breed has strong protective instincts but he is not inherently an aggressive breed – he is more likely to step back and assess the situation than to rush into an attack.

I would be remiss if I didn't say that, sometimes, this picture is accurate. Some Rottweilers do have an aggressive side and they certainly do have protective instincts. But what I want you to realize is that, as a dog owner, YOU can influence the way your dog turns out. Those Rottweilers who bark viciously at intruders, lunging against their restraints with rage in their eyes are not the end-all be-all of the Rottweiler breed. These dogs are this way because that is what their owners made them. If you mistreat a dog and teach it to be mean and aggressive, that is what he will become. But if you show kindness to a dog and teach him discipline and trust, he can become something entirely different. That is the challenge of training your Rottweiler.

Is the Rottweiler the Right Choice for You?

Now that you know a little more about the Rottweiler's temperament, exercise needs, and training challenges you may be forming a better picture of whether this is the right breed for you. Before you choose I encourage you to finish the rest of this book (and don't forget about other Rottweiler training books). I also want you to ask yourself the questions in this Rottweiler owner checklist – your answers will help you to determine if this is the right breed for you. Here you go:

Rottweiler Owner Checklist		
Do I have a large enough home to house a Rottweiler? (no condos or small apartments)	Yes	No
Do I have a fenced backyard or other safe outdoor space for my Rottweiler to play?	Yes	No

Do I have the time to devote to strengthening the bond with my Rottweiler?	Yes	No
Am I willing and able to start training my Rottweiler at a young age?	Yes	No
Can I commit to being patient and gentle with my Rottweiler as he learns?	Yes	No
Can I commit to feeding my Rottweiler a high-quality dog food?	Yes	No
Can I afford to take my Rottweiler to the vet twice a year for check-ups and vaccines?	Yes	No
Can I commit to keeping my Rottweiler for his whole life?	Yes	No

CHAPTER 5

Rottweiler Puppies For Sale—

Should You Buy a Rottweiler Puppy or Adopt a Rottweiler Dog from a Rottweiler Rescue?

B y now you probably have a pretty good idea whether a Rottweiler is in your future or not. If you have decided that you want to get a Rottweiler, your next step is to decide whether you want a Rottweiler puppy or an adult dog. Rottweiler pups are absolutely adorable, but they can also be quite a handful! Take the time to carefully consider your options before you go out and buy a Rottweiler puppy.

Should You Get a Rottweiler Puppy or Adult?

When you are ready to say that a Rottweiler is definitely your breed of choice, you still have one more decision to make – do you want a Rottweiler puppy or an adult dog? There are pros and cons of both these options, so think carefully and do your research before you make a definite decision. First, let's talk about the pros and cons of getting a Rottweiler puppy.

One thing that no one can debate is that Rottweiler pups are one of the most adorable things on the planet. Puppies in general are little more than cuddly bundles of love and Rottweiler puppies are that times a hundred. I can't accurately describe the joy of holding a Rottweiler puppy in your lap and having him fall asleep right there. But as cute and cuddly as that puppy is, he will also be a lot of work to take care of. Puppies are always getting into mischief, and you have to keep a close watch on them at all times. You'll also have to take on the challenge of training and socializing your puppy.

There is no denying that Rottweiler puppies are adorable but they are a challenge to raise – are you up to the challenge?

Training and socializing a puppy can be challenging, but it can also be very rewarding. If you want to have some control over how your Rottweiler turns out, you may be better off getting a puppy and doing the training and socialization yourself. Puppies are very malleable and impressionable – it takes time for their personalities to develop. If you want to make sure that your

Rottweiler gets along with other dogs and household pets, or that he gets along with children and other people, starting with a puppy might be the way to go.

Raising a puppy can be a lot of work, and some people simply aren't up to the task. If you don't think that you want to deal with the challenges of a Rottweiler puppy, consider adopting an adult dog. There are a variety of benefits that come with adopting an older dog. For one thing, adult dogs are more fully developed in terms of their personality and temperament. For the most part, with an adult dog, what you see is what you get. There is also a good chance that an adult rescue dog will already be housetrained and may have some obedience training under his belt. You are also probably going to pay less in adoption fees for an adult Rottweiler than you would for a puppy and the dog may already be spayed or neutered if you get him from a shelter.

Though these benefits of adopting an adult dog are great, there are some disadvantages to consider. For example, many dogs that end up in shelters come from bad living situations – they may already have behavioral problems or health issues that are not immediately apparent. Also, by adopting an adult dog, you may not be able to influence his personality and temperament as much as you can with a puppy. It is up to you to decide whether the pros outweigh the cons for an adult Rottweiler or a puppy.

To review the pros and cons of adult Rottweiler dogs versus Rottweiler puppies, consult the chart below:

Rottweiler Puppies	
Pros	**Cons**
Cute and cuddly	Can be destructive and mischievous
You can influence his personality/temperament	Personality may change as he grows/develops
You get to train him in whatever way you want	Training and socialization takes time and patience
May form a stronger bond	More expensive to buy a puppy and pay for vaccines and spay/neuter surgery

Adult Rottweiler Dog	
Pros	**Cons**
Personality is largely set, won't change much	May come from a bad living situation – could mean behavioral issues
Less worry about destructive "puppy" behavior	May have some bad habits that need to be addressed
Already house trained and may have some obedience training as well	You may not be able to influence his personality or temperament
May be spayed/neutered and caught up on vaccines	You miss out on cute puppy behavior

Buying Rottweiler Puppies for Sale vs. Adopting

Once you've decided whether you want an adult Rottweiler or a puppy, you then have to decide where you want to get him. You can buy Rottweiler puppies for sale from a breeder or you can go through a Rottweiler rescue. You could also consider a general dog rescue organization, though these organizations can't guarantee that they will have any Rottweiler dogs available for adoption at all, let alone Rottweiler puppies. For the most part, when puppies are surrendered to a shelter or rescue, they tend to be adopted out very quickly.

Whether you choose to buy a Rottweiler puppy or adopt an adult dog, do your research to find the option that is best for you.

If you are thinking about adopting a dog from a Rottweiler rescue, there are some things to think about. For one thing, you'll have to fill out an application with your contact

information, proof of residency, proof that you are allowed to
have pets at your residence and, in some cases, proof of income.
You have no guarantee that the shelter will approve your
application. The benefit, however, is that adoption fees are usually
much lower than buying Rottweiler puppies for sale from a
breeder.

On the other side of the coin, buying a Rottweiler from a breeder
means that you get to pick the exact puppy you want. Keeping in
mind that puppies will change a little as they grow and develop,
you will be able to influence a puppy's temperament a little more
than you would a dog who is already grown and matured. Plus,
the experience of raising and bonding with a puppy is unbeatable.
If, however, you choose to adopt an adult dog you should do some
research to find out how many dog shelters are in your area and
to determine if there are any local or regional rescue operations
that specialize in Rottweiler dogs.

CHAPTER 6

How to Avoid Buying Rottweiler Puppies in Puppy Mills

P uppy mills are a global problem and it is possible that as many as 10,000 puppy mills exist in the United States alone. In the United Kingdom, some statistics suggest that as many as one out of every three puppies that is sold came from a puppy mill. A puppy mill is a type of breeding operation in which profits are placed above the wellness and wellbeing of the dogs. Dogs are forced to breed continually, and they are kept in squalid conditions just so the owners can make an extra buck.

A puppy mill breeder dog is kept in a cage for most of its life. In many cases, those cages are barely big enough for the dog to move around, and they may even be forced to share it with other dogs. Cages are stacked on top of each other so feces and uneaten food falls down through the levels, creating a heartbreaking sight and a horrible odor. Adult dogs in puppy mills are often suffering from malnutrition and other diseases related to the deplorable conditions and as soon as they are no longer able to produce a litter, they are killed and replaced.

If you think that the area where you live is exempt from this kind of horror, think again. The American Kennel Club states that 1.8 million puppies are sold each year in the U.S. that come from puppy mills. Organizations like PETA and the Humane Society work to shut down puppy mills but for every puppy mill that is shut down, another (or more than one) rises to take its place. You can't always tell if a puppy comes from a puppy mill but, if you buy your puppy from a pet store or from someone who can't tell you exactly where the puppy came from (or who refuses to do so), it is probably a puppy mill puppy.

Think about how you would feel if your Rottweiler lived in a puppy mill. Now multiply that feeling by 100. That is how you should be feeling about the fact that puppy mills even exist.

So, what can you do to help reduce the number of puppy mills in existence? One thing is to refuse to support local pet stores that get their Rottweiler pups (and other puppies) from puppy mills.

Some pet stores only get their puppies from local shelters and rescue operations, but many don't. If the pet store can't (or won't) tell you exactly which breeder or organization the puppies came from, it is a very good possibility that they are the product of puppy mill breeding. Something else you can do to help support the crack-down on puppy mills is to contact your local legislators about your concerns.

CHAPTER 7

Rottweiler Breeders – How Do You Find a Good One?

For those of you who have chosen to go with a Rottweiler puppy, congratulations! You are going to love your new puppy so much – I know I did when I first got Rusty. But before you get caught up in the excitement, I want to talk to you about something very important – choosing the right breeder. There are plenty of Rottweiler breeders out there, but they are not all good. Some breeders don't do DNA testing for their breeding stock, which means that you could end up with Rottweiler puppies that are sick or carrying a serious disease.

Now, I don't want you to think that finding a responsible Rottweiler breeder is an impossible task – it isn't! But you should be prepared to put in some time and to do a little bit of research. Don't worry, I'll walk you through it!

Sifting Through Rottweiler Breeders to Find a Gem

When you are ready to start looking for reputable Rottweiler breeders, there are a few places you can start. It doesn't hurt to ask around at local pet stores and vet clinics to see if anyone can give you a referral to a Rottweiler breeder. Next, consult breeder lists provided by the American Kennel Club or the United Kingdom

Kennel Club. You may also find a local or regional Rottweiler breed club in your area that has a list of breeders. If all else fails, just do a search for "Rottweiler breeders" and see what comes up. Just don't buy a puppy from a website that ships puppies – these are usually stocked by puppy mills.

A responsible Rottweiler breeder won't have anything to hide – they will answer your questions and be glad to give you more information. That is the kind of breeder you can trust!

Once you've accumulated a list of Rottweiler breeders, take the time to go through your list and qualify each option. Start by checking the breeder's website to get a feel for their operation. Answer the questions, where is the breeder located? How long have they been breeding dogs? Do they hold any certifications or licenses? And don't forget to look for reviews and recommendations of the breeders on your list. If you can't find any information about them, remove them from your list and move on.

After you have gotten a little bit of information about each breeder (enough to determine whether they are worth considering), you'll need to shorten your list by deepening your investigation. Contact each breeder by phone and ask some questions – the answers they give will help you determine whether it is a responsible breeding operation or not. Here are some questions to ask:

- How long have you been breeding dogs? How long have you been breeding Rottweilers in particular?
- What do you love the most about the Rottweiler dog breed? What do you find challenging?
- What made you decide to start breeding Rottweiler dogs? Do you have any that you keep as pets?
- How do you choose your breeding stock? What kind of genetic testing do you do?
- Do your Rottweiler puppies for sale come with any kind of health guarantee or contract?
- How much do you charge for your puppies, and how much of a deposit do you require?

When you talk to each of the breeders on your list, record their answers to your questions. If you aren't satisfied with the answers a breeder gives, remove them from your list. Remember too that these breeders should be asking you questions about yourself because they want to make sure that their puppies go to good homes. After you've narrowed your list to two or three options, think about paying a visit to the breeding facilities to make sure that everything is in order. If you're happy with what you see, you can move on to talk about how to reserve a puppy.

To help you narrow down your list of options for Rottweiler breeders, use this breeder report card to record the results of your search:

Rottweiler Breeder Report Card		
Source:		
Certificate/License:		
Website:		
Phone Number:		
Years Experience:		
Health Guarantee?	YES	NO
Puppies Available?	YES	NO
Colors Available?	Blue	Gray
Deposit Required?	YES	NO
Notes:		

Picking Out a Healthy Rottweiler Puppy

Once you've done the work and have chosen the breeder you want to work with comes the fun part – picking out your puppy! Again, don't get too caught up in the excitement because you want to make sure that the puppy you bring home is in good health. If he doesn't start out healthy, you may find yourself dealing with a lifetime of expensive vet bills, not to mention the heartache of watching your puppy suffer. Here are some things you should do to pick out your puppy:

- Ask for a tour of the breeding facilities if you haven't already had one.
- Make sure that the breeding stock looks to be in good health - the breeder may even show you a health certificate or the results of DNA testing.
- Take a look at the Rottweiler puppies available to make sure they are ready to go home - if the puppies are under 8 weeks old, they should still be with the mother because they need to be fully weaned before separation.
- Stand back and observe the puppies for a while – watch how they interact with each other. Be on the lookout for red flags like lethargic behavior, visible wounds, evidence of diarrhea, aggressive or fearful behavior, etc.
- Wait for the puppies to notice you and let them come over when they are ready - let the puppies sniff and explore you for a minute or two before you bend down to interact with them.
- Play with the puppies a little, making mental notes about each puppy in terms of his activity level, curiosity, and personality.
- Take turns petting each puppy and picking them up to take a quick physical exam - observe how the puppy reacts to being picked up as well to see if he is calm and seems to enjoy being held or if he appears to be very frightened of you.
- Look at the puppy over for signs of illness like discharge from the eyes or nose, visible wounds, dry flaky skin, patchy coat, or masses under the skin.

After you've had a chance to observe and interact with the Rottweiler puppies and you feel like you are ready to make your decision, tell the breeder and put down whatever deposit may be required to reserve the puppy. Remember, a responsible breeder won't sell a puppy less than 8 weeks old, or one that hasn't been fully weaned. If the Rottweiler puppies are already weaned, you may be able to take your puppy home that very day.

CHAPTER 8

Your New Rottweiler Puppy—
How to Make Him Part of Your Family

While you may have already picked out your Rottweiler puppy, there is still more that needs to be done. You need to prepare your home and your family for the arrival of your new puppy. The first thing you need to do is purchase the supplies your puppy is going to need. Next, you'll have to make your home safe for puppy – this is called puppy-proofing. You'll also want to set up a special area in the house that your puppy can call his own.

What Supplies Will Your Puppy Need?

To meet your Rottweiler puppy's basic needs, you'll be needing some basic supplies. Here is a list of what you'll need:
- A crate or kennel
- A dog bed or blanket
- Food and water bowls
- Chew toys
- Interactive toys
- Puppy playpen
- Grooming supplies

Perhaps the most important thing your Rottweiler puppy is going to need is a small crate. There are some who think that confining a puppy to a crate is cruel, but I am a firm believer that if you condition your puppy to think of the crate as his own personal space, he will actually like being in it! The most important rule to remember is to never use the crate as punishment. During your first few days with puppy, make sure to incorporate the crate into your games and feeding time, so he gets used to it.

If you use it correctly, your Rottweiler will not fear his crate – he will think of it as his own little hideaway. A place to call his own where he can take a nap, or just have a little bit of time to himself.

When it comes to picking out your puppy's crate, keep in mind that it should only be big enough for your puppy to comfortably stand up, sit down, turn around, and lie down in. The idea here is that if your puppy's crate is only large enough for him to sleep in that he will come to think of it as his den. Dogs have a natural aversion to soiling their den and cultivating this feeling will help with housetraining. You can also line the crate with a bed or blanket to make it more comfortable for your Rottweiler puppy.

After your puppy's crate comes his food and water bowls. The important thing here is to pick something durable, like stainless steel. Not only is stainless steel incredibly lightweight and durable, but you don't have to worry about it scratching or harboring bacteria like softer materials such as plastic. If you don't like the look of stainless steel, ceramic is another good option – just be sure that the bowls aren't too large for your puppy to use easily.

Next, come your puppy's toys. You'll want to start out with an assortment of different options so you can get a feel for what your puppy likes. Choose a few different kinds of chew toys to give your puppy an outlet for his natural desire to chew and be sure to invest in some interactive toys. These will give your puppy some mental stimulation, and it will keep your puppy from getting bored. I can tell you from experience – a bored puppy is a destructive one.

In addition to your puppy's crate, you'll also want a puppy playpen that you can use to confine him without keeping him in the crate. You'll put your puppy's crate and all his stuff in the playpen to create his own little area. Put the playpen in a room where it won't be in the way but where it won't be completely isolated either. When your puppy is housetrained, you may be able to put the playpen away and just keep his crate, bowls, and toys in the area, so he has access to them.

Finally, you'll need some supplies such as a collar, leash, and harness as well as your dog's grooming supplies. For grooming supplies, you'll need a wire-pin brush with short bristles, and you may also want a shedding rake. For your puppy's collar, it needs to be sized appropriately which means that you'll have to buy several as your puppy grows - or you can start with an adjustable collar.

Your Rottweiler puppy will need lots of toys to help him work off his energy and to channel his desire to chew. Don't skimp!

You may also want to think about a harness for your Rottweiler puppy. While a collar is perfectly fine, there are some risks involved. When a strong dog like the Rottweiler pulls on the leash and his owner pulls back, it can cause the collar to strain against his neck, which could damage his windpipe. A harness helps to distribute the pressure from the leash across your puppy's back instead of concentrating it around his neck. It can also give you a little more control when your Rottweiler is fully grown and very strong.

Keeping your Rottweiler Puppy Safe – Puppy Proofing

Once you have set up your Rottweiler puppy's special area, you need to go through the rest of the house to make sure it is safe. Basically, you just want to remove or put away anything that could be hazardous. Here are some things that you should think about when puppy-proofing your house for your Rottweiler:

- Put away all your cleaning products as well as any household chemicals you have – put them in a cabinet that closes tightly or locks.

- Cover up or put away open food containers – take them off the counter and put them in your cupboard or pantry.

- Cover all your trash cans with tight-fitting lids or put them in a cabinet to keep your puppy out of them.

- Be sure to pick up all small objects off the floor and put them away where they belong (or get rid of them if you don't need them).

- Coil up electrical cords and blind cords so they don't dangle where your Rottweiler puppy can get them.

- Make sure that all medications and bathroom toiletries are stowed away safely in a cabinet.

- Be sure to cover up or drain any open bodies of water (like the bathtub and the toilet), so your puppy doesn't fall in by accident.

- Check to be sure that none of your houseplants are poisonous - put all plants out of your puppy's reach.

- Do what is necessary to close off your fireplace (if you have one), and make sure that all doors and windows stay tightly closed.

- Be sure that your puppy can't hurt himself on the furniture – try to dull or cover sharp edges and keep an eye out for rocking chairs.

- Make use of baby gates or pet gates to keep your Rottweiler puppy out of areas that could be dangerous - also, keep him away from the stairs.

- For cat owners, make sure the litter box is kept somewhere your puppy can't reach– the same for pet food besides your puppy's own food.

- Clean up small clothing items (like socks and hosiery), and keep them out of your puppy's reach.

- Carefully dispose of food waste like fruit pits, vegetable peels, bones, etc.

There are always more things you can do to keep your home safe for your Rottweiler puppy. What you may want to consider doing is walking around your house while viewing things from your puppy's perspective (you might even crawl around!). Anything that looks tempting to chew on or play with that isn't completely safe should be removed or put away.

CHAPTER 9

Rottweiler Food—
Your Rottweiler Dog's Nutritional Needs

D o you think that buying dog food is as simple as going to the pet store and just picking something off the shelf? While this may technically be true, I'm here to tell you that it isn't that simple. All dog food is not created equal and the product you choose for your Rottweiler will have a significant impact on his health and wellness. If you buy the cheapest dog food available, you might save money on the food, but you'll probably end up spending more in vet bills throughout your dog's life. If your Rottweiler's diet doesn't provide the nutrients he needs, he can't possibly be healthy.

What Nutrients Does Your Rottweiler Need?

First and foremost, your Rottweiler needs a balance of protein, fat, and carbohydrate in his diet. Protein is the most important of these for dogs because dogs are carnivores. That means that their bodies are adapted to digesting and utilizing nutrients from animal-based foods, not plants. Proteins are made up of amino acids and there are 22 different kinds. Your dog's body can make 12 of them, but the remaining 10 amino acids must come from your dog's diet, and they are called essential amino acids for this reason. Dogs require a minimum of 18% protein in the diet of adult dogs and 22% for puppies. The best protein sources for dogs are meats like poultry, beef, and fish.

The next most important nutrient for Rottweilers is fat. Though you may think that fats are bad, they are loaded with the essential fatty acids needed to help to maintain your dog's skin and coat, but it is also the most highly concentrated source of energy available to dogs. The fat in your dog's food should come from animal-based sources and it should make up a minimum of 8% a Rottweiler puppy's diet and at least 5% an adult dog's diet. Plant-based fats can be used in a supplemental way to balance out the omega-3 and omega-6 fatty acid content of your dog's diet.

Take your time when shopping for your Rottweiler's food because it will be his primary source of nutrition – choose something that is properly balanced and loaded with healthy proteins.

In terms of carbohydrates, your dog doesn't have specific requirements but they need to be digestible. Carbohydrates provide your dog with usable energy and dietary fiber but a diet that is too carbohydrate-heavy can be bad for him. At most, your dog's diet should contain 5% dietary fiber and any carbs in his diet should also come from highly digestible sources like whole grains or fresh fruits and veggies. Be careful, though, because some dogs are sensitive to grains – especially grains like corn, wheat, and soy which offer very little nutritional value for dogs. These are also some of the most common food allergens. Whole grains like brown rice, oatmeal, and pearled barley are better in terms of nutrition for dogs but they can still cause problems for those that suffer from food allergies or sensitivities.

How to Read a Dog Food Label

Now you know what kind of nutrients your dog needs, but how do you pick a product that will provide for those needs? First, you'll need to learn how to interpret the information on a pet food label. Basically, there are three things you should pay attention to: the AAFCO statement of nutritional adequacy, the guaranteed analysis, and the ingredients list.

Let's start with the AAFCO statement of nutritional adequacy. Basically, the American Association of Feed Control Officials (or AAFCO) is responsible for regulating the production and manufacture of pet foods as well as animal feed. In simple terms, AAFCO pretty much does for pet food what the USDA and the FDA do for human foods. To determine whether a pet food product is complete and balanced for dogs, they created nutrient profiles for adult dogs and for puppies to determine the minimum nutritional requirements. Before a product can be sold, AAFCO compares it to those minimum requirements and if the product meets those requirements, it is called "complete and balanced".

Remember, the AAFCO statement doesn't say whether a product is high-quality or not – it just means that the product meets your dog's minimum nutritional requirements by life stage.

When you look at a pet food label, you want to look for this AAFCO statement which tells you that the product will meet your Rottweiler's basic needs. Remember, however, that this statement is not a guarantee of quality – you also must check the ingredients and the guaranteed analysis. The guaranteed analysis is the part of the label that tells you how much crude protein, fat, and fiber is in the product. Compare those crude values to the minimum requirements for dogs that you learned about in the last section to see whether the product sticks pretty close to the bare minimums or if it exceeds them.

After checking the guaranteed analysis, your next place to look is the ingredients list. The first thing you need to know is that ingredients lists are ordered in descending order by volume – the things that are listed at the top are used in the highest volume. This being true, you want to see a high-quality meat protein, as the first ingredient since protein is the most important nutrient for dogs. Any dog food that lists a plant-based ingredient first should be avoided.

After you've checked the first ingredient, read the rest of the top 10. You want to see other sources of protein as well as healthy fats and digestible carbohydrates. It is generally better to see animal-based ingredients higher on the list than the plant-based ingredients, but each product is different. Also, pay attention to the things that are NOT listed. Avoid dog foods made with by-products as well as anything made from corn, wheat, or soy. Rottweiler food products that are heavy with plant proteins (like pea protein or potato protein) are generally bad signs, such as using tainted food from underdeveloped countries in order to cut costs.

Feeding Tips for Rottweiler Puppies and Adult Dogs

When it comes to Rottweiler puppy food and adult Rottweiler food, nutritional balance is very important. But you also need to be mindful of how much you are feeding your dog. Your dog's energy needs will vary depending on certain factors like as age, weight, sex, and activity level.

Rottweiler puppies need a lot of energy and protein to fuel their growth and development, so it is best to choose a dog food that is formulated for medium to large-breed puppies. You might be okay with a regular puppy formula but be mindful of the fat content because excess fat can cause your Rottweiler puppy to grow too fast, and that is dangerous for large-breed dogs because it increases their risk for musculoskeletal problems when they grow up.

Whatever recipe you chose for your Rottweiler puppy food, be sure to follow the feeding instructions on the label – recommendations are made based on your puppy's age and weight. You might be able to let your Rottweiler puppy feed freely while he is very young if he can ration himself, but if he starts to grow too fast you may want to switch to portioning out his meals. Weigh your puppy at least once a week and talk to your vet if you are concerned about his rate of growth.

When your Rottweiler puppy reaches about 80% of his expected adult size, you should think about switching to an adult recipe – ideally a large-breed adult recipe. These Rottweiler dog foods are high in protein and moderate in fat content – this helps to prevent your dog from getting too many calories. Remember, however, that if you train your Rottweiler dog sports his energy needs may be higher. Again, just follow the feeding recommendations based on your dog's age, weight, and activity level for several weeks and keep track of his weight. If he gains too much weight you can cut back a little bit and if he loses weight or energy, you can increase his portion a little bit.

Dangerous Foods to Avoid

Though it can be tempting to give in to your Rottweiler when he begs for table scraps, you need to be very careful about feeding him "people food". Many of the same foods that you eat daily can be very dangerous for your Rottweiler. Here is a list of potentially harmful foods to avoid feeding your dog:

- Alcohol/beer
- Apple seeds
- Avocado
- Cherry pits
- Chocolate
- Coffee
- Garlic
- Grapes/raisins
- Macadamia nuts
- Mold
- Mushrooms
- Mustard seeds
- Onions/leeks
- Peach pits
- Potato leaves/stems
- Rhubarb leaves
- Tea
- Tomato leaves/stems
- Walnuts
- Xylitol
- Yeast dough

CHAPTER 10

Rottweiler Health – Common Conditions Affecting Rottweilers

All dogs are more or less susceptible to certain health problems – the Rottweiler is no exception. Not only do Rottweilers have a shorter lifespan than some other large-breed dogs, but they are also prone to a good number of diseases. The best way to protect your dog against these diseases is to get him vaccinated (if there is an applicable vaccine) and to learn as much as you can about them. The more you know, the sooner you can identify a problem and the sooner your dog can get treatment.

What Conditions Are Common in Rottweilers?

For health problems affecting the Rottweiler breed, there are a few categories to consider. For musculoskeletal issues, Rottweilers are prone to hip and elbow dysplasia, osteochondritis, and intervertebral disc disease. For other issues, Rottweilers may be prone to gastric torsion, hypothyroidism, colitis, von Willebrand's disease, and progressive retinal atrophy.

The best way to protect your Rottweiler from these problems is to learn as much as you can about them. Learning the basics about various health conditions known to affect the Rottweiler breed can help you to identify symptoms as soon they manifest. The sooner you notice symptoms, the sooner you will be able to have your vet make a diagnosis, and the sooner your Rottweiler can begin treatment. Keep reading to learn the basics about common health problems affecting the Rottweiler dog breed.

If you want to protect your Rottweiler from disease you should take the time to learn about its risks – the more you know, the sooner you can identify a problem and seek treatment.

Hip and Elbow Dysplasia

Musculoskeletal issues are fairly common in large-breed dogs, especially if they grew too quickly as puppies. Two orthopedic issues which are particularly common in Rottweilers are hip dysplasia and elbow dysplasia. Hip dysplasia happens when the head of the dog's femur bone slips out of its intended position (luxates) in the hip socket. This luxation can cause both pain and stiffness in the rear legs, as well as worsening arthritis as the problem progresses. Elbow dysplasia is similar in many ways but it usually results from a defect in the front legs that the puppy may be born with. This defect causes the head of the humerus to slip out of place. Both of these musculoskeletal conditions can be corrected surgically, though many vets prefer to treat minor cases with anti-inflammatories and other medical management options.

Osteochondritis

Also known as osteochondritis dissecans, this is a problem affecting the Rottweiler's joints (particularly the elbows, shoulders, and hocks). In most cases, symptoms first start to manifest between 4 and 6 months of age, and they may be the result of inadequate growth. If the bone ends do not grow at the same time, or if they become misshapen, it can cause problems with the synovial fluid that is supposed to lubricate the joints. Without this lubrication, the bones can split, and small pieces of bone may lodge in the joint space, causing your dog a lot of pain. In most cases, surgical correction is needed but is not always successful.

Intervertebral Disc Disease

Your Rottweiler's spine is made up of small bones that are called vertebrae and they are all connected by discs made up of a cartilage-like substance. When one of these discs becomes weak or damaged, it may protrude from the disc space – this is called a herniated or ruptured disc and it is the hallmark of intervertebral disc disease (IVDD). Symptoms of IVDD include intense pain in the middle of the back – your dog may also become reluctant to move his head. Your dog might start shivering from the pain and may exhibit changes in his gait – he may even become paralyzed. In mild cases, IVDD can be managed medically but if your dog has multiple episodes, surgery may be recommended to permanently correct the issue.

Rottweilers are a stoic breed so they may hide their pain if something hurts – it's your job to know your dog well enough that you notice changes in behavior that could indicate a problem.

Gastric Torsion

Another problem that affects large-breed dogs like the Rottweiler more than smaller breeds is called gastric torsion or gastric dilatation volvulus. This condition develops when the dog's abdomen fills with air which causes the stomach to twist on its axis. This twisting cuts off blood supply to the stomach and to other vital organs – this problem can escalate quickly and may result in an emergency situation. Without immediate veterinary care, most dogs die of this condition. To help prevent bloat from harming your Rottweiler, keep him from eating or drinking large quantities at once, especially after exercise.

Hypothyroidism

This condition is caused by inadequate thyroid hormone production in the thyroid gland. Though this condition may be caused by physical damage to the thyroid gland, it is more frequently caused by autoimmune activity, cancer, or overuse of certain medications. In many milder cases where the deficiency remains small, there may not be any noticeable symptoms. Still, the dog will require lifelong treatment with synthetic thyroid hormone. In more severe cases where symptoms do manifest, you may notice signs like thinning coat, coarse or brittle hair, lethargy, drooping eyelids, mental dullness, unexplained weight gain, and irregular heat cycles in female dogs. Hypothyroidism usually affects dogs 4 through 10 years of age and it requires lifelong treatment.

Colitis

This is a condition affecting the dog's colon which is characterized by chronic inflammation. The colon is simply another name for the large intestine and it is the part of the digestive tract where indigestible fibers are turned into stools for excretion. If your dog's colon fails to do its job properly, it may be the result of inflammation, or colitis. Symptoms of colitis usually involve diarrhea. Problems with the colon can be brought on by stress, dietary problems, or a sudden change in diet. Certain medications may help to control symptoms and you might have to start being more careful with your Rottweiler's diet.

Your Rottweiler is your best friend so you should do everything you can to keep him in good health – that means keeping an eye out for symptoms of disease and getting treatment when needed.

Von Willebrand's Disease

This is a type of inherited blood disorder which can lead to problems with clotting. Dogs with von Willebrand's Disease (vWD) have an insufficiency of von Willebrand Factor (vWF) which is necessary for clotting. If a dog with vWD gets a cut or some other minor injury, it may bleed profusely – some dogs also experience frequent nosebleeds or bleeding gums. Some dogs even develop internal bleeding, which can be diagnosed by blood in the urine. If your Rottweiler has vWD, you'll need to be especially careful any time he undergoes surgery – he may need a blood transfusion.

Progressive Retinal Atrophy

There are a number of eye conditions to which the Rottweiler may be prone, but progressive retinal atrophy (PRA) is one of the most common. This is a progressive disease, which means that it will continue to get worse over time, and it generally affects the dog's retinas. In the early stages of PRA, your dog may develop problems with his night vision. As the condition progresses, he may lose his daytime vision as well, and the lens of the eyes may become cloudy, resulting in the formation of a cataract. Rottweilers usually start to show signs of PRA between 2 and 5 years of age, and, in most cases, they are completely blind within a year. Fortunately, most dogs adapt well to the loss of their sight, and PRA is not a painful condition.

What Vaccinations Does Your Rottweiler Need?

While giving your dog a healthy diet and keeping up with regular vet check-ups will go a long way toward preserving his health, there is something else you should do - get him vaccinated. As a puppy, your Rottweiler needs certain vaccines every 6 to 12 weeks during his first year of life. After that first year, most vaccines only need to be given as an annual booster. The vaccines your dog needs depend on his age and where you live – your veterinarian will be able to tell you what your dog needs.

To give you an idea exactly which vaccines your Rottweiler might need and when he will need them, here is a schedule for dog vaccinations:

Vaccination Schedule for Rottweilers			
Vaccine	**Doses**	**Age**	**Booster**
Rabies (US only)	1	12 weeks	annual
Distemper	3	6-16 weeks	3 years
Parvovirus	3	6-16 weeks	3 years
Adenovirus	3	6-16 weeks	3 years
Parainfluenza	3	6 weeks, 12-14 weeks	3 years
Bordetella	1	6 weeks	annual
Lyme Disease	2	9, 13-14 weeks	annual
Leptospirosis	2	12 and 16 weeks	annual
Canine Influenza	2	6-8, 8-12 weeks	annual

CHAPTER 11

Rottweiler Training –
Everything You Need to Know
About Training Rottweilers

As much as I adore my Rusty, our first few months together were a little rough. Don't get me wrong – I've never regretted getting him for one second, but if I had known that training a Rottweiler might be so challenging I would have done a little more preparation upfront – that is what I'm encouraging you to do. In this book, I'm going to give you a basic idea of what to expect during Rottweiler training and give you some tips to train Rottweiler puppies. But I would encourage you to do some extra research with other Rottweiler training books to give yourself the best chance for success.

The Dos and Don'ts of Rottweiler Training

Before you dive head-first into Rottweiler puppy training, I'd like to give you some idea what you can expect. Training a puppy is never easy – they are so full of energy and excitement that it can be hard to harness that energy and put it toward training. This is particularly true of intelligent breeds like the Rottweiler. They want to learn, but they also want to have fun, so make sure that your Rottweiler training sessions incorporate both!

First and foremost, start training your Rottweiler puppy as early as you can. You may not be able to teach a 3-month old puppy to roll over or fetch the newspaper, but you can lay the groundwork for training by teaching him the house rules. Are you going to let your puppy jump up on the couch? Are you going to let him whine for food at the dinner table? Decide what things you are and are not going to allow your dog to do and then start enforcing those rules as soon as you bring your puppy home.

Training a Rottweiler is by no means an easy task,
but with patience and firm, consistent leadership, you can be successful.

Something else you need to understand about Rottweilers is that these dogs can be a bit dominant at times. Dominant doesn't necessarily mean aggressive – it simply means that your dog may have a strong personality and a bit of an independent side. I wholeheartedly oppose the kind of dominance training that Cesar Milan (The Dog Whisperer) advocates, because it involves punishment and putting your dog down. I think that the best way to deal with a potential dominance problem is to simply position yourself as the alpha of the household. Be firm and consistent with your training, but never be mean.

Finally, you need to be patient with Rottweiler puppy training. I personally recommend that you start training your puppy around 6 weeks of age – definitely no later than 5 or 6 months. During the early stages of training it may be frustrating when your puppy doesn't catch on to something as quickly as you would like or when he backslides and starts to exhibit a particular behavior that you thought you had under control. All I can tell you is that patience wins – when you are firm and consistent with your dog but also patient, he will learn to respect and trust you and that is the key to Rottweiler training.

Crate Training Your Rottweiler Puppy

One of the first things you'll need to do as part of your Rottweiler puppy training is crate training. If you remember earlier, I told you that confining a puppy to his crate is not cruel if you go about it the right way. First, you have to get your puppy used to the crate, so he doesn't become afraid of it. As long as you use the crate properly (and not as a form of punishment), your puppy will come to view it as his own special place where he can take a nap or just get away from the family for a while. This feeling is going to play an important role in housetraining your Rottweiler puppy.

Crate training is not difficult – all you need is some time, a lot of treats, and plenty of praise. The underlying secret to achieving success with crate training is to teach your dog that you like it when he does his business outdoors. Rottweilers can become very attached to their owners, and they have a natural desire to please. So, if you can teach your Rottweiler that it pleases you when he does his business outdoors and not in the house, he will be eager to repeat that kind of behavior.

Your Rottweiler wants nothing more than to please you, so make sure you praise and reward him for following your commands!

When housetraining your Rottweiler puppy, you'll need to have a crate to keep him in when you can't watch him. If you follow advice from an earlier chapter, you'll have a special area set up for your puppy where you can keep him contained without keeping him in his crate.

You'll want to wait until he's a little older and at least partially housetrained to do this. Now, follow these steps to properly crate train your Rottweiler puppy:

1. Take your puppy outside at least once every hour or two. He will also need to go immediately after waking from a nap, before going to bed at night, and about 30 minutes after a meal.

2. When you take your Rottweiler puppy outside, always take him to the same location so he learns that is where you want him to do his business.

3. When he does his business in that area, give him a treat and praise him excitedly, so he knows that you approve. You can also try giving him a verbal command like "Go Pee" when you take him to his spot – eventually you'll be able to just open the door, give him the command, and he'll know what to do.

4. When you are at home with your puppy, keep him in the same room with you at all times, and keep a watch for signs that he has to go.

5. If your puppy starts to sniff the ground, turn in circles, or squat, it is time to pick him up and rush him outside.

The key to housetraining is supervising your puppy when he is awake and keeping him in his crate while he is asleep. By doing these simple things you can drastically reduce the risk for accidents in the house. Just be as consistent as possible with giving your puppy chances to go outside and never force him to hold his bladder for longer than he is able. Puppies can only control their bladder and bowels for about 1 hour per month of age, plus one. That means that a two-month old Rottweiler puppy can only hold his bladder for a maximum of about 3 hours.

When you do it correctly, housetraining your Rottweiler puppy is surprisingly easy! Just be patient and consistent with the puppy.

Positive Reinforcement and Click Training Rottweilers

After crate training, obedience training is the next most important aspect of training your Rottweiler puppy. If you follow the steps from the last section, you'll already be a little familiar with positive reinforcement training. Remember the part about giving your puppy a treat when he does his business outside? That's what I'm talking about! Positive reinforcement training involves rewarding your puppy for doing things you want him to do, and not rewarding him for things you want him to stop doing. Because the Rottweiler is an intelligent breed, he should pick up on things pretty quickly – it may only take 3 or 4 repetitions for him to learn a new command.

 ou an example of what positive reinforcement training looks like, here are the steps you would follow to teach your puppy to sit:

1. Kneel in front of your Rottweiler puppy and pinch a small training treat in your fingers.

2. Hold the treat in front of your puppy's nose and let him get a good whiff of it.

3. Tell your puppy to "Sit" in a firm tone of voice.

4. Immediately after issuing the command, move the treat forward and up toward the back of your puppy's head.

5. Your puppy will respond by raising his nose to follow the treat and, in doing so, his bottom will lower to the ground.

6. As soon as your puppy's bottom touches the floor, tell him "Good!" and give him the treat.

7. Repeat this sequence a few times until your puppy starts to respond to the command without you moving the treat.

See, positive reinforcement training is easy! You just have to teach your dog what you expect when you give him a certain command and then reward him for following it. If you want your puppy to learn even faster, you might consider incorporating a clicker. Clicker training is just another type of positive reinforcement training and it can help your dog identify the desired behavior more quickly. With regular positive reinforcement training, when your dog exhibits the proper response, you immediately praise him and reward him to reinforce it. With clicker training, you click a little sound maker as soon as your dog performs the desired behavior, which helps him to identify it more quickly. This is proven to be an effective technique, so well worth trying.

CHAPTER 12

Rottweiler Grooming:

How to Control Shedding and Keep Your Rottweiler Looking His Best

One of the most identifiable characteristics of the Rottweiler breed is their black-and-tan coats. Rottweiler dogs are uniquely beautiful with their coloration but their lovely coats do require some maintenance. As a dog owner, it is part of your responsibility to care for your dog's coat. Not only does that mean providing him with the right nutrients to nourish his coat, but you must also brush and bathe him as needed, to keep his skin and coat in good condition.

Grooming your Rottweiler includes more than just taking care of his coat. You won't have to worry about trimming your dog's coat because it doesn't grow very long, but you should keep it clean. You'll also have to care for your Rottweiler's ears, teeth, and nails. In is chapter, you'll learn the basics about grooming your Rottweiler from head to toe.

What is the Rottweiler's Coat Like?

The Rottweiler is known for his muscular build and for his black-and-tan coat. The majority of your dog's coat will be black, but he should have rust-colored markings on the sides of his muzzle, over each eye, and on his cheeks. He may also have markings on his chest and legs. Each Rottweiler is unique in the size, placement and shade of his markings, but most Rottweilers are very similar in terms of their appearance.

The Rottweiler is easy to identify by his muscular build and his black-and-tan coat with specific markings.

Rottweilers have a double coat, which means that they have a soft, short undercoat with a longer top coat. The top coat is medium-length on most of the body but shorter on the head, ears, and legs. The texture of the top coat may be slightly harsh and coarse to the touch. This double coat protects your Rottweiler from cold weather which is why many Rottweilers do just fine as outdoor dogs, as long as they have shelter. This doesn't mean, however, that you can just leave your dog outside all the time – Rottweilers need attention and companionship as much as any dog.

Brushing and Bathing the Rottweiler

The Rottweiler's coat is medium-length and it sheds an average amount – about the same as most dog breeds. Any Rottweiler savvy dog owner will tell you, however, that the key to controlling shedding is frequent brushing. Rottweiler dogs should be brushed at least once a week to remove loose hair and to help distribute the natural oils produced by your dog's skin to help keep in soft and healthy. Your dog may shed more heavily twice a year with the changing seasons, so be prepared to do some extra brushing during those times. Rottweilers only need to be bathed a few times a year when they get particularly dirty.

Brushing your Rottweiler's coat is not difficult, and all you really need is a wire pin brush and maybe a slicker brush for the undercoat. A slicker brush is a flat brush with small bristles that can reach into your dog's undercoat. To brush your dog's coat, start at the back of his head at the base of his neck and then gently work your way down the back and sides – always move the brush in the direction of hair growth. The Rottweiler's coat is medium in length, but generally still short enough that you shouldn't have to worry about tangles and mats. Next, work your way down each leg then get his belly and chest.

If your Rottweiler gets particularly dirty, you can give him a bath. Start by filling the bathtub with a few inches of warm water (not hot) and have your Rottweiler step into it. Use a handheld sprayer or a cup to thoroughly wet down your dog's coat, then use a small amount of dog-friendly shampoo and work it into a lather. Once he's all soaped up, rinse him off well enough to remove all traces of soap. Be careful to avoid getting your Rottweiler's face or ears wet, because dampness in the ears can become a breeding ground for bacteria. If you need to clean your dog's face and head, use a damp washcloth. To dry your Rottweiler, just use a large towel. If he will allow it, you may also be able to use the blow-dryer on the lowest heat setting.

Some Rottweilers love getting baths, while others do not.
Start your puppy early to make sure he gets used to it.

Other Rottweiler Grooming Tasks

Though brushing your Rottweiler's coat is your main grooming task, you also need to care for his teeth, ears, and nails. Rottweilers have flop ears, which means that the ears hang down on either side of the dog's head. Because the ears hang down, they get less air flow than erect ears (called prick ears) which may increase your dog's risk for ear infections. You need to keep your Rottweiler's ears clean and dry at all times, and clean them every few weeks, as needed.

To clean your Rottweiler's ears, you just need some dog-safe ear cleaning solution and cotton balls or pads. First, squeeze a few drops of the dog-safe ear cleaner into your Rottweiler's ear canal and then carefully massage the base of his ear to distribute the solution. Next, use a clean cotton ball or cotton pad to remove ear wax as well as any debris and excess solution. Finally, let your dog's ears air-dry. It only takes a few minutes to clean your dog's ears, but it goes a long way toward preventing ear infections.

In addition to cleaning your Rottweiler's ears, you also need to take care of his teeth. Your best bet is to start early – Rottweiler puppies that get used to having their teeth touched early will be more amenable to regular brushing. Start getting your Rottweiler puppy used to having his face, mouth, and teeth touched. It is best to use your fingers at first, and then gradually work your way up to using a dog-safe toothbrush. Once your Rottweiler puppy has gotten used to the toothbrush you can then add a little bit of dog-friendly toothpaste. At first you should only brush a few teeth at a time then slowly work your way up to brushing all the top teeth or all the bottom teeth in one session. Eventually, you should be brushing his teeth every day.

The final grooming task you'll need to perform on a regular basis, is trimming your Rottweilers nails. This is an easy task but you do need to be careful because the nail contains a blood vessel called the quick – it provides the blood supply to the nail and if you cut your dog's nail too short, you could sever the quick. This will not only be painful for your dog but it will likely cause profuse bleeding as well. What you want to do is trim the minimum amount from your Rottweiler's nails every week or two to prevent them from growing too long.

CHAPTER 13

Rottweiler Life Expectancy and Caring for Senior Dogs

D ogs are more than just pets – they are members of the family. As your family grows and changes, so does your Rottweiler. My own Rusty has been my faithful friend and companion for more than 5 years now, and I couldn't imagine my life without him. Unfortunately, the harsh reality of life is that Rusty won't always be around. Dogs simply don't live as long as humans do, and that's why we must appreciate them and love them as much as we can while they are here with us.

All pet owners dread the fact that, inevitably, their last day with their dog is going to come sooner than they would like. Unlike humans, dogs always live in the moment- it is the only thing they know. But even so, they also live their lives in fast-forward, aging more quickly than we do. A very lucky dog will live to 15 years, maybe even 20. But large-breed dogs like the Rottweiler usually aren't so lucky. This breed has an average lifespan of just 8 to 10 years, which is tragically short. It just means that you really have to take advantage of every moment you have with your dog because your moments are numbered and time passes more quickly than we would like to admit.

To give you an idea of just how quickly your Rottweiler will age compared to you, consider this age chart:

Calendar Year	Rottweiler Age Equivalent
1 Year	15
2 Years	24
3 Years	30
4 Years	35
5 Years	42
6 Years	48
7 Years	53
8 Years	59
9 Years	65
10 Years	71
11 Years	77
12 Years	83

Although the Rottweiler's average lifespan is just 8 to 10 years, there are no guarantees for how long he will live – his lifespan will be influenced by several different factors. For one thing, breeding is important – if your Rottweiler was poorly bred (whether he inherited any congenital diseases) it could seriously reduce his longevity. Any diseases or health problems your Rottweiler experiences throughout his life can also play a role in shortening his lifespan.

One of the most significant factors in determining your Rottweiler's longevity is the quality of his diet. Like humans, dogs need specific nutrients in their diet and if they don't get those nutrients, they won't be healthy. In the moment, it might seem like buying a cheaper, lower quality dog food is not a problem but it could lead to problems like nutritional deficiencies or other diet-related diseases that could shorten your dog's lifespan and lead to some expensive vet bills.

As your Rottweiler gets older, he may slow down a bit, but he will still be the beautiful, loving friend that you've bonded with over the years.

As your Rottweiler ages, you'll need to make some accommodations to keep him comfortable. Because Rottweilers only live about 10 years, they may technically be considered a "senior" dog around 6 years. Throughout his life, you should take your dog to the vet twice a year for check-ups. Once he reaches senior status, however, you might want to consider going a little more often. Regular check-ups are the key to catching diseases and other health problems in the early stages when they are still treatable. Your dog's immune system may weaken as he ages, so he won't be able to fend off infections and other health problems as easily.

Another thing you should do for your senior Rottweiler is help to keep him comfortable around the house. You should consider investing in an orthopedic pet bed to keep him off the cold floor and to support his aging bones and joints. If your Rottweiler has joint problems, consider giving him glucosamine and chondroitin supplements. You might also try a senior dog food formula (ideally one formulated for large-breed dogs). You should also make sure your dog doesn't spend too much time in extremely hot or cold temperatures and think about getting a ramp or set of stairs to help him into the car and onto the bed.

CHAPTER 14

Should You Show Your Rottweiler?

The Basics About Dog Shows

When you think about the Rottweiler breed, you probably don't picture him in the center of a dog show ring. Of course, not every Rottweiler is right for showing but it may be something you want to consider. Preparing your Rottweiler for show is definitely not easy, but it can be a very rewarding experience. Not only will it give you and your dog a chance to spend more time together, but it can help you to strengthen your dog's obedience and discipline. Before you decide to show your Rottweiler, however, you should learn the basics about dog shows.

What are the Benefits of Dog Shows?

Many dog owners assume that participating in a dog show is only worth it if their dog wins. While it can be a matter of pride to have your dog perform well, that is not the only reason that you might consider training your Rottweiler for show. Only one dog can win the coveted "Best in Show" title but there are other rewards for participating in the competition for both you and your dog. For example, a dog show is a fun activity that can become an excellent opportunity for you and your dog to spend time together.

Not only are dog shows fun, but preparing for a dog show is great as well. Your dog will need to be properly trained and disciplined to do well in the show – that means that you'll have to work with him on your own time. The time you spend training for the show is just more time that you get to share with your dog, strengthening your bond with him. The time you spend at the show is also a great chance to network with other dog owners, and your Rottweiler might even make some new friends!

The Rottweiler is a beautiful and intelligent breed that can do very well in the show circuit with proper training and discipline.

Tips to Prepare for Your First Show

One of the most important things you want to remember going into your first dog show is that winning isn't everything. While it is certainly possible that your Rottweiler could win during his debut show, it is unlikely. It takes years for the best dog trainers to train and condition their dogs for show and it will take you some time as well to learn the ins and outs of competition. The more often you and your Rottweiler compete, however, the more quickly you will learn, and you may see your dog rising in the ranks rather quickly.

To help you get the most out your first dog show with your Rottweiler, consider the following tips:

- Do not feed your Rottweiler too much on the day of the show – you want your dog to be just hungry enough that he will perform for food during the show.

- Make sure you arrive at the show at least an hour early so you have time to set up your space, walk your dog, and get your bearings.

- Always keep your Rottweiler in his crate when he isn't doing his business or performing - you want him to be in tip-top shape for judging so you'll need to keep his coat clean.

- Prepare your dog early so he is ready to go at least a few minutes before his appointed show time – you want to be able to hand your dog off to the handler when it's his turn.

- Don't forget to take a lot of pictures! You should also take notes about your experience to use in preparing for your next show.

- Always keep a positive mindset throughout the show experience - even if your dog doesn't do well you can learn from your mistakes for next time!

Most importantly, don't forget to have fun! A dog show can be an exciting challenge for both you and your dog, but it should also be fun! Don't waste a single minute.

CHAPTER 15

Thinking of Breeding Rottweiler Dogs? What You Need to Know

The first time I set eyes on my Rusty, I didn't think that anything in the world could be cuter. Many dog owners feel this way about their own Rottweiler puppies, which leads them to consider an interesting option – breeding their dog. Breeding your dog could yield an entire litter of cute, cuddly Rottweiler puppies, and that sounds like a good thing, doesn't it? I'll admit, the thought of a letter of roly-poly Rottweiler puppies sounds amazing, but I want you to consider the practical implications of breeding your dog before you decide to do it. Rottweiler breeders don't become breeders on a whim – they think about it carefully, and they make a commitment to doing it right – so should you.

Things to Think About Before Breeding Your Dog

Many people assume that breeding dogs is as simple as putting a male and a female dog in the same room together. While this is technically true, there is a great deal more time and preparation that goes into the process – at least if you want to be a responsible breeder, it does. Choosing to breed your Rottweiler is not something you should do on a whim. Breeding is not a risk-free situation for dogs and you also must consider that you may end up being responsible for the care of an entire litter of Rottweiler puppies, at least until they are ready to go to new homes.

Rottweiler puppies are roly-poly bundles of fur. They start off remarkably small but quickly grow into big, muscular dogs!

In addition to thinking about the practical aspects of breeding your Rottweiler, you also need to learn the basics about dog breeding in general and what you will need to make it happen. First and foremost, you are going to need two Rottweilers – a male and a female. But you can't choose just any dog. You'll want both dogs DNA tested to see if they are carriers for certain inherited health conditions like hip dysplasia or various heart defects. If either of the dogs is a carrier, he or she should not be bred. You'll also want to choose dogs that have a gentle temperament – don't breed a dog that has aggressive tendencies.

After you've chosen your breeding stock, you want to make sure that they are in excellent condition for breeding. This means feeding your dogs a high-quality and nutritious diet as well as having them checked out by a vet. If your female Rottweiler is in less than optimal condition, the strain of the pregnancy could become dangerous. Throughout the gestation period you'll need to keep a close eye on her health with regular vet check-ups. As she approaches her due date, she may need more food and you'll have to make some practical preparations for whelping.

Once your Rottweiler puppies are born, you may think that the hard part is over, but that isn't the case – you are just getting started. Not only will you be responsible for the care of your post-partum female dog, but you will also responsible for the growth and development of a litter of Rottweiler puppies. Rottweilers have a fairly large average litter size – it is not uncommon for them to have 10 to 12 puppies at a time. Are you ready to care for a dozen Rottweiler puppies in addition to your adult dog? You'll need to care for those puppies for at least 8 weeks until they are weaned and ready to be separated from their mother.

The Basics of Dog Breeding

Now that you have a general understanding of what will be expected of you if you breed your Rottweiler, you need to learn the basics of how dog breeding really works. As a medium-large breed, the Rottweiler may take a little longer than some dogs to reach sexual maturity. Male Rottweilers may reach sexual maturity as early as 6 to 9 months of age, though the generally don't reach their full size until 12 months or more. Female Rottweilers can become sexually mature around 6 months in rare cases, but most don't become mature until 12 to 18 months.

The sign that a female Rottweiler is sexually mature is her first heat cycle. The heat cycle is another name for the estrous cycle, the biological cycle through which a female dog becomes capable of and receptive to breeding. If a female dog goes into heat and is successfully mated to a fertile male dog, the female will become pregnant, and the gestation period will begin. The gestation period is simply the period of time during which the fetuses develop inside the female's body. The gestation period for most dogs lasts about 63 days, or 9 weeks.

The average litter size for Rottweiler puppies is about 6, though it is not uncommon for litters to contain 10 to 12 puppies!

The heat cycle in female Rottweilers usually lasts for about three weeks and, once your dog matures, the cycle occurs every 4 to 6 months. Some female Rottweilers will become very regular and frequent with their cycles, while others may have just one cycle a year. The first stage of the cycle is called proestrous, and it lasts for an average of 9 days. This is the part of the cycle when your female Rottweiler will start bleeding. During this stage, she will be very attractive to male dogs, but she is not ready for breeding – you'll need to keep her inside and separated from other dogs.

As the cycle continues, your Rottweiler will go into the second stage – estrous. This stage lasts about 9 days, and during this period your dog will become receptive to mating and capable of becoming pregnant. If you mate your female to a fertile male and she becomes pregnant, the gestation period will begin. While the Rottweiler puppies grow inside their mother's womb, your female dog will need to start eating a little bit more to support the growth and development of the puppies. In most cases, you can just leave a bowl of food for your female dog, and she will eat as much as she needs. Near the end of the gestation period, your female Rottweiler might be eating two or three times as much as she was prior to pregnancy.

When the end of the gestation period starts to approach, you may notice your female Rottweiler becoming restless. By this time, you should have provided a whelping box in a quiet, dimly lit location where your dog can give birth in peace. Do everything you can to keep your Rottweiler comfortable at this time, but be aware that labor is just as painful for dogs as it is for humans. Try to soothe your dog by petting her gently and make sure that she knows you are by her side. When your dog is ready to give birth, her water will break, and she will begin whelping the puppies – they usually come about 10 minutes apart.

While your Rottweiler puppies are growing, make sure that they feed several times a day and make sure they stay warm.

After all of the Rottweiler puppies have been born, your female will clean the puppies and they will start nursing. Your dog may clean each puppy immediately after birth, or she may wait until the end. If she doesn't bite the umbilical cord herself to sever it, you can cut it yourself with a pair of sharp scissors. Don't interfere with the puppies too much, but make sure that they start feeding within about an hour of being born. The first milk your female Rottweiler produces is called colostrum, and it contains valuable antibodies your puppies will need to protect them while their immune systems develop.

The puppies will spend most of their time sleeping and feeding during the first few weeks until they grow big enough to move around and to start sampling solid food. Once the puppies' eyes and ears open, they will also start to play with each other. Your female Rottweiler will probably naturally begin to wean the puppies after 4 to 5 weeks, and they should be fully weaned around 7 to 8 weeks of age. Do not separate the Rottweiler puppies from their mother until they are completely weaned.

CHAPTER 16
Conclusion

At this point, you should have a thorough understanding of the Rottweiler breed. What do you think now? Do you think these dogs are as wonderful as I do? We all have our own preferences, but I hope that you've come to recognize the unique beauty of the Rottweiler breed. These dogs are lovely – both inside and out – and they remain one of my favorite breeds to this very day. I hope you feel the same!

As much time as I've spent telling you how amazing the Rottweiler dog breed is, I do want to make sure I don't neglect to paint an accurate picture of what it is like to own one of these dogs. A properly trained and socialized Rottweiler makes an excellent family pet – he will be gentle with children and amenable to other dogs and household pets. But a Rottweiler is not an easy dog to raise. In addition to being a very large breed, Rottweilers are very intelligent, and they need plenty of opportunities to use their brains. Your dog won't be content to lay on the couch all day.

If you think you are ready to bring home a Rottweiler puppy, I want you to ask yourself whether you are ready to make a 10-year commitment. Though some Rottweilers live just 8 years, most live to 10 and some live longer. Unless you are able to care for your Rottweiler for his entire life, you should not become a dog owner. You also need to decide whether you are able to take the time to train and socialize your Rottweiler from an early age. This is no minor commitment of time and effort – it takes a lot of work to develop a feisty Rottweiler puppy into a well-behaved and mild-mannered adult.

The Rottweiler is a wonderful breed, but I don't want you to just take my word for it – take the time to learn for yourself!

If, after reading this book you think that the Rottweiler is not the right choice for you, there's nothing wrong with that!

As much as I adore my Rusty, he is definitely not the easiest dog to work with sometimes. A Rottweiler (or any dog, really) is a major commitment – you don't get to take time off from being a dog owner!

Thanks for taking the time to read this book – I hope that you have come to adore the Rottweiler breed as much as I do! If you have even the slightest feeling that the Rottweiler is a breed worth considering, I feel that I have done my job correctly. I don't want to just tell you that the Rottweiler is a great dog – I want you to come to that conclusion on your own. So, in closing, I want to wish you good luck and Godspeed with your Rottweiler!

Useful Terms to Know

AKC – American Kennel Club, the largest purebred dog registry in the United States

Almond Eye – Referring to an elongated eye shape rather than a rounded shape

Apple Head – A round-shaped skull

Balance – A show term referring to all the parts of the dog, both moving and standing, which produce a harmonious image

Beard – Long, thick hair on the dog's underjaw

Best in Show – An award given to the only undefeated dog left standing at the end of judging

Bitch – A female dog

Bite – The position of the upper and lower teeth when the dog's jaws are closed; positions include level, undershot, scissors, or overshot

Blaze – A white stripe running down the center of the face between the eyes

Board – To house, feed, and care for a dog for a fee

Breed – A domestic race of dogs having a common gene pool and characterized appearance/function

Breed Standard – A published document describing the look, movement, and behavior of the perfect specimen of a particular breed

Buff – An off-white to gold coloring

Clip – A method of trimming the coat in some breeds

Coat – The hair covering of a dog; some breeds have two coats, and outer coat and undercoat; also known as a double coat. Examples of breeds with double coats include German Shepherd, Siberian Husky, Akita, etc.

Condition – The health of the dog as shown by its skin, coat, behavior, and general appearance

Crate – A container used to house/transport dogs; also called a cage or kennel

Crossbreed (Hybrid) – A dog having a sire and dam of two different breeds; cannot be registered with the AKC

Dam (bitch) – The female parent of a dog;

Dock – To shorten the tail of a dog by surgically removing the end part of the tail.

Double Coat – Having an outer weather-resistant coat and a soft, waterproof coat for warmth; see above.

Drop Ear – An ear in which the tip of the ear folds over and hangs down; not prick or erect

Entropion – A genetic disorder resulting in the upper or lower eyelid turning in

Fancier – A person who is especially interested in a particular breed or dog sport

Fawn – A red-yellow hue of brown

Feathering – A long fringe of hair on the ears, tail, legs, or body of a dog

Groom – To brush, trim, comb or otherwise make a dog's coat neat in appearance

Heel – To command a dog to stay close by its owner's side

Hip Dysplasia – A condition characterized by the abnormal formation of the hip joint

Inbreeding – The breeding of two closely related dogs of one breed

Kennel – A building or enclosure where dogs are kept

Litter – A group of puppies born at one time

Markings – A contrasting color or pattern on a dog's coat

Mask – Dark shading on the dog's foreface

Mate – To breed a dog and a bitch

Neuter – To castrate a male dog or spay a female dog

Pads – The tough, shock-absorbent skin on the bottom of a dog's foot

Parti-Color – A coloration of a dog's coat consisting of two or more definite, well-broken colors; one of the colors must be white

Pedigree – The written record of a dog's genealogy going back three generations or more

Pied – A coloration on a dog consisting of patches of white and another color

Prick Ear – Ear that is carried erect, usually pointed at the tip of the ear

Puppy – A dog under 12 months of age

Purebred – A dog whose sire and dam belong to the same breed and who are of unmixed descent

Saddle – Colored markings in the shape of a saddle over the back; colors may vary

Shedding – The natural process whereby old hair falls off the dog's body as it is replaced by new hair growth.